Read for a Better World™

MEGALODON

A First Look

HANNAH GRAMSON

Lerner Publications ◆ Minneapolis

Educator Toolbox

Reading books is a great way for kids to express what they're interested in. Before reading this title, ask the reader these questions:

What do you think this book is about? Look at the cover for clues.

What do you already know about megalodons?

What do you want to learn about megalodons?

Let's Read Together

Encourage the reader to use the pictures to understand the text.

Point out when the reader successfully sounds out a word.

Praise the reader for recognizing sight words such as *they* and *as*.

TABLE OF CONTENTS

Megalodons

Megalodons were sharks. They lived three million years ago.

Megalodon
Whale shark
Great white shark

They were the biggest sharks ever.

They were as long as one or two school buses!

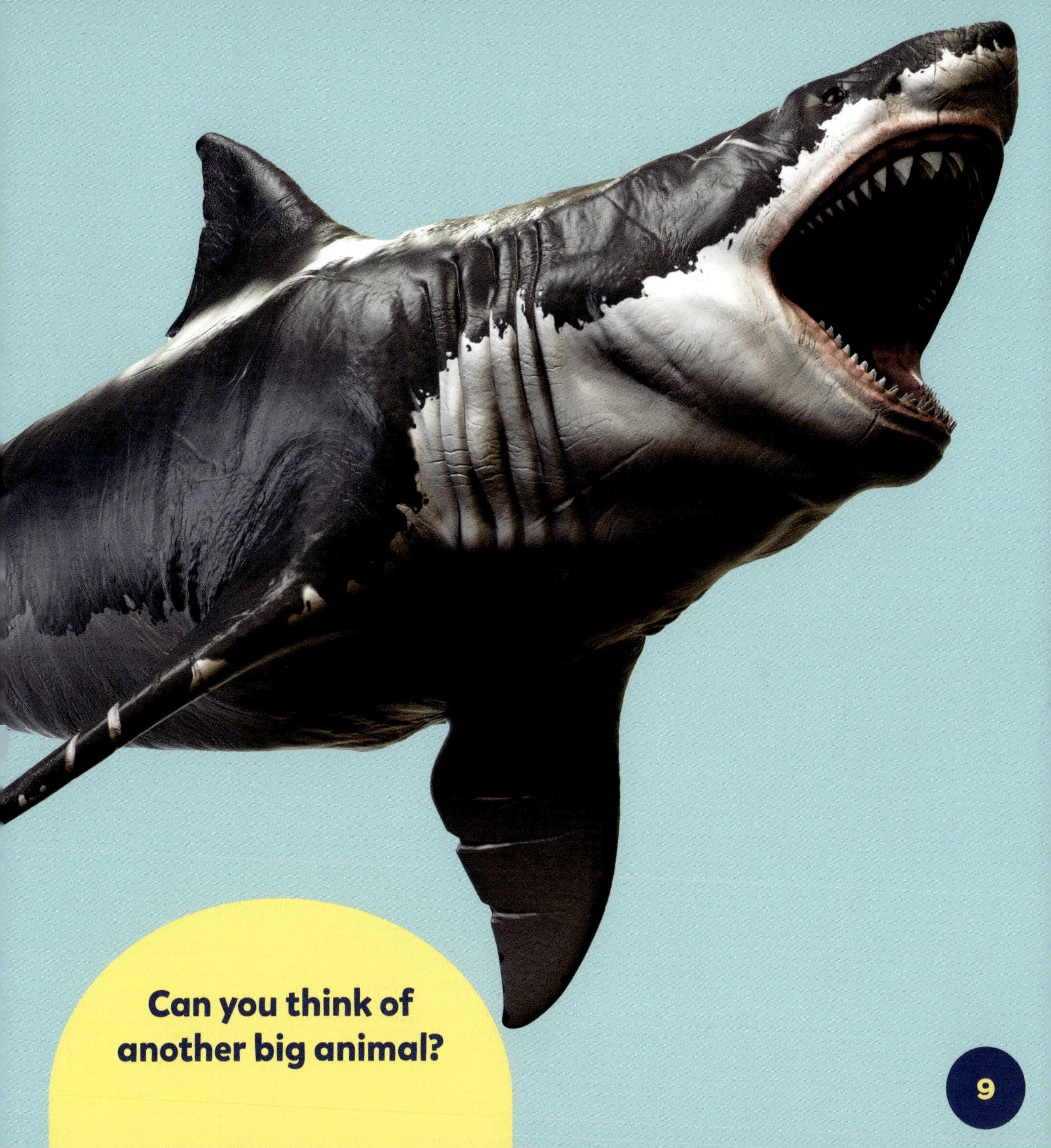

Can you think of another big animal?

They lived in oceans.

They ate whales and seals.

They could open their jaws wide.

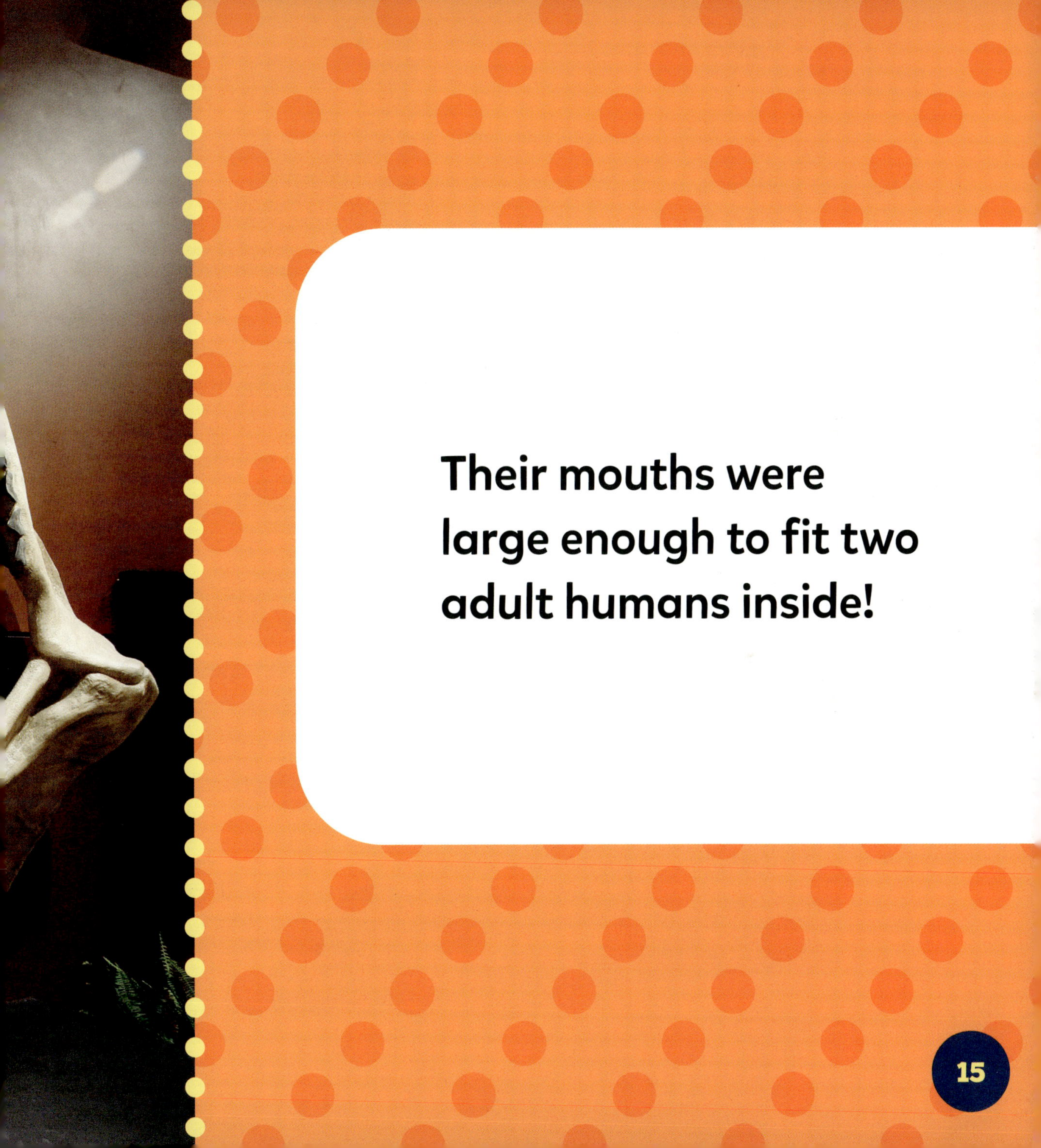

Their mouths were large enough to fit two adult humans inside!

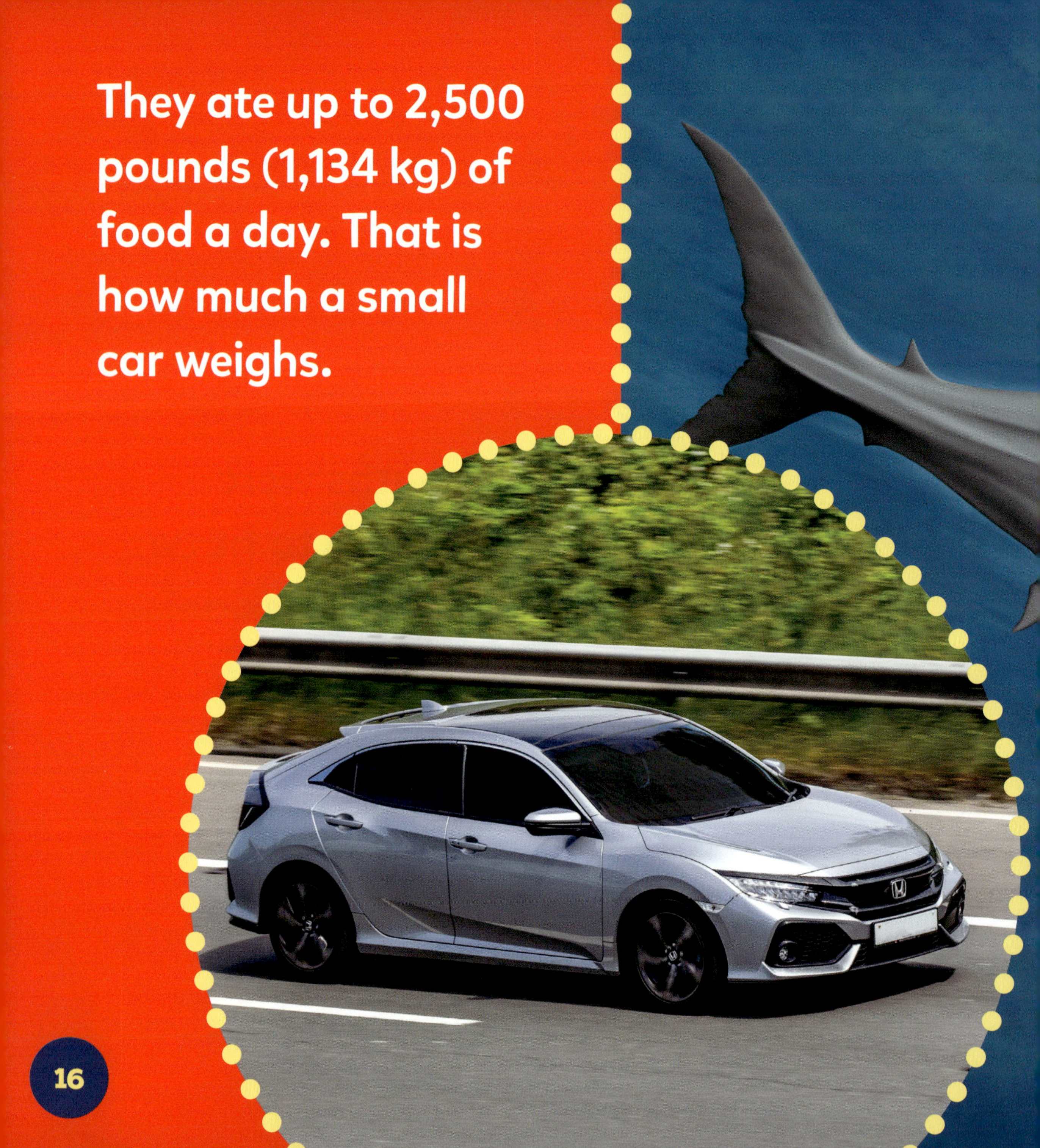

They ate up to 2,500 pounds (1,134 kg) of food a day. That is how much a small car weighs.

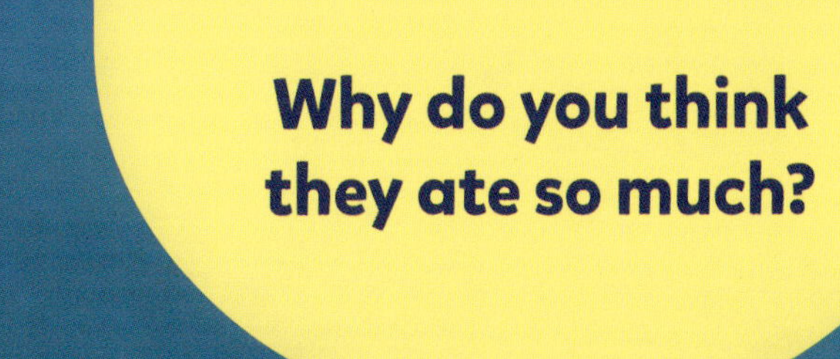
Why do you think they ate so much?

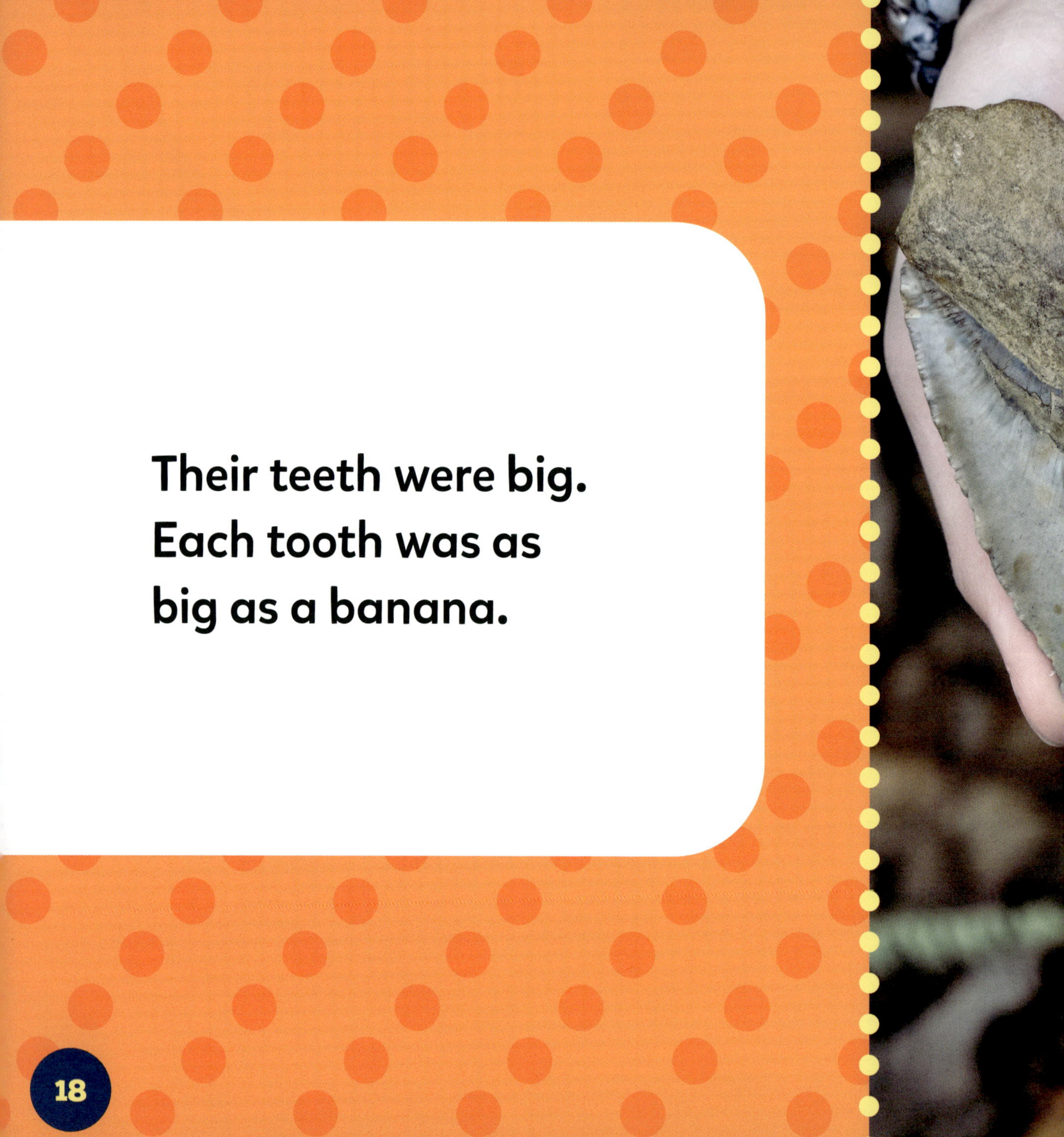

Their teeth were big.
Each tooth was as
big as a banana.

How were their teeth helpful?

Not much remains of megalodons. People learned about these sharks by looking at their teeth.

You Connect!

What do you like about megalodons?

Would you want to meet a megalodon?

What other sea animals would you like to learn about?

STEM Snapshot

Encourage students to think and ask questions like scientists. Ask the reader:

What have you learned about megalodons?

What have you noticed about the way megalodons looked?

What do you still want to learn about megalodons?

Photo Glossary

Learn More

Leed, Percy. *Sharks: A First Look*. Minneapolis: Lerner Publications, 2023.

Murray, Julie. *Mosasaurus*. Edina, MN: Dash! Leveled Readers, 2025.

Riggs, Kate. *Sharks*. Mankato, MN: Creative Education and Creative Paperbacks, 2025.

Index

Photo Acknowledgments

Image credits: Corey Ford/Stocktrek Images/Getty Images, pp. 4–5; Maquiladora/Shutterstock, pp. 6–7; typhoonski/Getty Images, p. 8 (bottom); Herschel Hoffmeyer/Shutterstock, pp. 8–9; Elenarts/Shutterstock, p. 10; Douglas Klug/Getty Images, p. 11; Gabriele Holtermann/Sipa USA via AP Images, pp. 12–13; Ethan Miller/Getty Images, pp. 14–15; ZarkePix/Alamy, p. 16 (bottom); martinspurny/Getty Images, pp. 16–17; Mark Kostich/Getty Images, pp. 18–19; AlessandroZocc/Getty Images, p. 20.
Cover: Herschel Hoffmeyer/Shutterstock.

Copyright © 2026 by Lerner Publishing Group, Inc.

All rights reserved. International copyright secured. No part of this book may be reproduced, stored in a retrieval system, or transmitted in any form or by any means—electronic, mechanical, photocopying, recording, or otherwise—without the prior written permission of Lerner Publishing Group, Inc., except for the inclusion of brief quotations in an acknowledged review.

Lerner Publications Company
An imprint of Lerner Publishing Group, Inc.
241 First Avenue North
Minneapolis, MN 55401 USA

For reading levels and more information, look up this title at www.lernerbooks.com.

Main body text set in Mikado Medium.
Typeface provided by Hannes von Doehren.

Editor: Annie Zheng **Photo editor:** Lucien Brinkley

Library of Congress Cataloging-in-Publication Data

Names: Gramson, Hannah, author.
Title: Megalodon : a first look / Hannah Gramson.
Description: Minneapolis : Lerner Publications, [2026] | Series: Read about prehistoric beasts (read for a better world) | Includes bibliographical references and index. | Audience: Ages 5–8 | Audience: Grades K–1 | Summary: "Millions of years ago, megalodons swam Earth's oceans. They were the largest sharks to ever live! Young readers will enjoy discovering fun facts about these prehistoric beasts, from what they ate to how they looked"– Provided by publisher.
Identifiers: LCCN 2024044227 (print) | LCCN 2024044228 (ebook) | ISBN 9798765669051 (library binding) | ISBN 9798765684696 (paperback) | ISBN 9798765680377 (epub)
Subjects: LCSH: Carcharocles megalodon—Juvenile literature. | Marine animals, Fossil—Juvenile literature. | Paleontology—Neogene—Juvenile literature.
Classification: LCC QE852.L35 G73 2026 (print) | LCC QE852.L35 (ebook) | DDC 567/.3—dc23/eng/20250103

LC record available at https://lccn.loc.gov/2024044227
LC ebook record available at https://lccn.loc.gov/2024044228

Manufactured in the United States of America
1-1011832-53876-1/21/2025